CELEBRATING THE CITY OF SÃO PAULO

Celebrating the City of São Paulo

Walter the Educator

Silent King Books

Copyright © 2024 by Walter the Educator

All rights reserved. No part of this book may be reproduced in any manner whatsoever without written per- mission except in the case of brief quotations embodied in critical articles and reviews.

First Printing, 2024

Disclaimer

This book is a literary work; the story is not about specific persons, locations, situations, and/or circumstances unless mentioned in a historical context. Any resemblance to real persons, locations, situations, and/or circumstances is coincidental. This book is for entertainment and informational purposes only. The author and publisher offer this information without warranties expressed or implied. No matter the grounds, neither the author nor the publisher will be accountable for any losses, injuries, or other damages caused by the reader's use of this book. The use of this book acknowledges an understanding and acceptance of this disclaimer.

Celebrating the City of São Paulo is a little collectible souvenir book that belongs to the Celebrating Cities Book Series by Walter the Educator. Collect them all and more books at WaltertheEducator.com

USE THE EXTRA SPACE TO TAKE NOTES AND DOCUMENT YOUR MEMORIES

SÃO PAULO

In the heart of Brazil, where dreams and concrete entwine,

Celebrating the City of São Paulo

Lies São Paulo, a city where modernity and history combine.

Skyward it stretches, a realm of towers and light,

A metropolis pulsing from dawn until night.

In avenues broad, the lifeblood flows fast,

Cars, buses, and bikes, a mechanical cast.

From Ibirapuera's greens to Paulista's grand street,

São Paulo's essence is a rhythm, a beat.

In the market of Mercadão, vibrant and alive,

Mangoes, spices, and coffee, senses revive.

Amidst the chatter of vendors and buyers,

Celebrating the City of São Paulo

A mosaic of faces, São Paulo never tires.

Liberdade's lanterns, a touch of the East,

A bridge between cultures, a visual feast.

Sushi and samba, harmoniously blend,

In São Paulo, every stranger's a friend.

The art of MASP, suspended in air,

Bold lines and colors, a canvas laid bare.

Graffiti whispers on walls of the town,

Street art in alleys, a visual crown.

The hum of the subways, beneath the stone streets,

Carries the tales of the city's heartbeat.

From Sé to Consolação, stories unfold,

Of dreams pursued and fortunes bold.

In Vila Madalena, where bohemian souls roam,

Bars and galleries, a creative home.

Celebrating the City of São Paulo

Music spills out, jazz and bossa nova,

In São Paulo, every night is a nova.

The flavors of Italy in Bixiga's embrace,

Pastas and laughter, a warm, welcoming place.

Brazilian churrasco, a carnivore's delight,

In São Paulo, food is a dance every night.

In the favelas, resilience stands tall,

Stories of struggle, of rising from fall.

Hope finds its way through narrow lanes,

In São Paulo, every heart's refrain.

Celebrating the City of São Paulo

Football fields, the passion ignites,

Corinthians and Palmeiras, legendary fights.

In stadiums vast, the cheers ascend,

In São Paulo, loyalty knows no end.

ABOUT THE CREATOR

Walter the Educator is one of the pseudonyms for Walter Anderson. Formally educated in Chemistry, Business, and Education, he is an educator, an author, a diverse entrepreneur, and he is the son of a disabled war veteran. "Walter the Educator" shares his time between educating and creating. He holds interests and owns several creative projects that entertain, enlighten, enhance, and educate, hoping to inspire and motivate you. Follow, find new works, and stay up to date with Walter the Educator™

at WaltertheEducator.com

www.ingramcontent.com/pod-product-compliance
Lightning Source LLC
LaVergne TN
LVHW010622070526
838199LV00063BA/5230